Emma Lea's Tea With Daddy

Written by Babette Donaldson • Illustrated by Jerianne Van Dijk
Published by Blue Gate Books, Nevada City, California

Copyright © 2009 Babette Donaldson
Illustration Copyright © 2009 Jerianne Van Dijk

All rights reserved. No part of this book may be reproduced or transmitted in any form or by any means except for the purpose of review, without written permission of the publisher.

Requests for permission to make copies of any part of the work should be mailed to:
Blue Gate Books
P.O. Box 2137
Nevada City, CA 95959
(530) 478-0365

Summary: Emma Lea prepares a special tea for her father.

ISBN: 978-0-9792612-3-7

[1. Juvenile Fiction 2. Tea 3. Father-Daughter 4. Children's Tea]

Library of Congress Control Number: 2009903706

Printed in China

Blue Gate Books
P.O. Box 2137
Nevada City, CA 95959

Design and computer production by Patty Arnold
Menagerie Design and Publishing www.menageriedesign.net

I dedicate this to my parents and brothers.
Bernice, Bill, Bobby, Bert & Blaine

As soon as Mama left with her friends for a day hike, Daddy started his fix-it-up projects. He showed Emma Lea the list of chores.

"I'd rather have a tea party, Daddy. Just you and me."

"Like you have with Theodosia Teddy Bear?"
He pretended to hold a teacup with his pinky finger pointing in the air.

She knew he was teasing.
"Not a playtime tea. A real tea.
Like Mama and me."

"Sounds tea-licious. But first,
I'll finish these jobs."

"OK," she said, "while you do that,
I'll make a tea party lunch."

"Can you do it by yourself?"
Daddy looked surprised.

"Everything except boil the water.
You can help with that."

Emma Lea wanted to make it extra-special for Daddy. She set the table in the living room with the blue tablecloth Mama had embroidered. Then she rolled the matching napkins into butterfly rings that she and Mama made as a rainy day project.

Grammie had always said that it was important to serve family memories with tea. So, she chose their teacups from the collection in the cupboard. Each one had a story. Daddy would use one that Grammie gave Mama for their wedding. She would use one that Grampop had made on his potter's wheel.

Emma Lea waved to Daddy through the window.

"Next, I'll hang your bike rack."

"OK, Daddy. I still have a lot to do."

She washed her hands and started planning the menu, Grammie's recipe for Cambric Spiced Tea and some of the tea cookies she and Mama baked yesterday.

Making fruit salad would be fun. She found bananas, strawberries, grapes and peaches which were soft enough to cut with a table knife. Then she didn't need to use anything sharp.

The sandwiches were easy. She called them Triple Butter Sandwiches. The bread was spread with three things – peanut butter, apple butter and honey butter.

She used cookie cutters to make them fancy. It was easy to turn every-day food into party food.

She was proud to be able to do it all by herself.

Emma Lea picked flowers from the garden for the centerpiece of their table. She could hear Daddy singing in the garage. It was their favorite silly song, "Would you like to swing on a star, carry moonbeams home in a jar . . ."

She sang along.

"Hey, Emmie," he called.
"There's one last chore I need to do."
He pushed the lawn mower out
into the tall grass. "I hope you don't
mind waiting a few more minutes."

"That's OK, Daddy. I'm still making
your surprise."

Emma Lea had time to change into her favorite dress and tie her braids with ribbons. She liked to dress up. It made the day seem more important. She hoped Daddy would remember this as one of their special times together.

This was the first time she had made lunch all by herself. But she knew she was doing just fine. She arranged the plates of sandwiches, fruit and cookies on the table and filled the kettle with cold water and set it on the stove.
Daddy would light the burner and pour the water when it was hot.

"What's this?" he asked when he saw her dress.

"It's my tea party dress," she answered.

Daddy looked at his dirty work clothes. "I should wash up and change my clothes too."

While Daddy was getting ready, Emma Lea decorated a name card for each of them.

He returned looking very handsome and proud. "Oh, my goodness," he exclaimed. "This is love-a-Lea." She liked the way he made up rhymes for her name.

He lighted the fire under the kettle while she explained what they would do next.

"I'll fix the tea," she said. "Half milk and half tea." She poured carefully and then stirred it with a whole cinnamon stick. "Daddy, would you like honey?"

"Yes, please," he answered.

"What shall we do at our tea party?" Daddy asked "Do we sing and read poems like you do at Grammie's?"

"We can just talk. I can tell you about what's been happening at school. You can tell me about your work or what you did when you were a little boy. You know. Things that matter."

Their stories lasted throughout the afternoon and a whole pot of tea.

Emma Lea and Daddy were still sitting at the table when Mama came home.

"Look what the two of you have done. This is lovely."

"Our daughter did this all by herself," Daddy replied. "And she's been teaching me the most important thing about tea parties."

"Spending time together!" shouted Emma Lea.

Rooibos Tea Cookies
Makes 12—18 cookies

1 teaspoon Rooibos herbal tea leaves

1/4 cup boiling water

1/2 cup buttermilk

1/2 cup butter, softened

3/4 cup brown sugar, packed

1 egg

2 teaspoons orange zest

2 cups all-purpose flour

1 teaspoon baking powder

1/4 teaspoon baking soda

1/4 cup powdered sugar (optional)

Infuse the Rooibos with the boiling water. Cover the cup and allow it to sit until completely cooled.

Preheat oven to 350°

In a large bowl, cream together the butter and 3/4 cup brown sugar until light and fluffy. Beat in the egg,. Then stir in the Rooibos and buttermilk. Combine the flour, baking powder and baking soda. Fold dry ingredients into the creamed mixture. Drop by rounded spoonfuls onto the un-greased cookie sheets.

Bake for 8 to 10 minutes in the preheated oven, until the edges are light brown. Allow cookies to cool on baking sheets for 5 minutes before transferring to a wire rack to cool completely.

Dusting with powdered sugar is decorative and optional.

Photo by Christian Koszka

Author

BABETTE DONALDSON is the author and creator of the Emma Lea stories. She has a BA in Creative Writing and a BFA in Ceramic Art from San Francisco State University and received her tea certification from the Specialty Tea Institute, the education division of The Tea Council of the United States. She is currently the director of Tea Suite, a non-profit organization supporting art education.

Designer

PATTY ARNOLD is the owner of *Menagerie Design and Publishing*—a small company specializing in book production. She has a BFA in sculpture and printmaking, a BS in Graphic Communications and an MFA in Photography and Digital Imaging. She also teaches Graphic Design, Typography, Animation and Digital Arts at the local community college and is an exhibiting photographer. You can view her fine art at www.pattyarnold.com and her design projects at www.menageriedesign.net.

Illustrator

JERIANNE VAN DIJK—An artist for over 30 years, Jerianne Van Dijk's award-winning illustrations have graced calendars, greeting cards, product labels, posters and books. She is proficient in various media and is as happy doing botanicals as goofy whimsical things to make you think. Jerianne began working as a graphic designer for an array of advertising agencies, newspapers, and printing companies. She particularly enjoys freelance illustration as one of her many specialties. Residing in Northern California as a watercolor instructor, fine artist and illustrator Jerianne enjoys the work her gift affords her. For more about her work visit www.jerianne.net

OTHER EMMA LEA BOOKS:

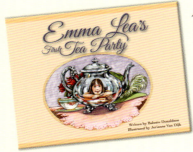

Emma Lea's First Tea Party
Emma Lea is excited to attend the annual tea party with the ladies of her family. They celebrate Grammy's birthday with a special dress up event.

Hardcover:
ISBN: 978-0-9792612-0-6 • $16.95

Emma Lea's Magic Teapot
When Daddy reads the bedtime story, Aladdin's Magic Lamp Emma Lea dreams her new teapot can also grant her three magical wishes.

Hardcover:
ISBN: 978-0-9792612-1-3 • $16.95

Emma Lea's First Tea Ceremony
Emma Lea's friend Sam invites her to tea at his home, Japanese style. She learns the most important elements of their tradition; Tranquility, Purity, Harmony & Respect.

Hardcover:
ISBN: 978-0-9792612-1-3 • $16.95

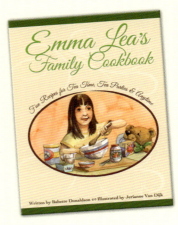

Emma Lea's Family Cookbook
This is a collection of 100 recipes from The Emma Lea Stories including the hardbound storybooks, the online Magic Teapot Stories and the Tea-Zine, Emma Lea's Virtual Tea Party. The recipes are based on family favorites, teatime traditions, nursery rhyme themes and having fun with food.

Soft cover:
ISBN: 978-0-9792612-4-4 • $16.95

Additional Emma Lea stories, activities and teacher's aids can be found at the website:
www.emmaleabooks.com